William I. Hull

Maryland, Independence and the Confederation

A paper read before the Maryland historical society, December 8th, 1890

William I. Hull

Maryland, Independence and the Confederation
A paper read before the Maryland historical society, December 8th, 1890

ISBN/EAN: 9783337180454

Printed in Europe, USA, Canada, Australia, Japan

Cover: Foto ©ninafisch / pixelio.de

More available books at **www.hansebooks.com**

MARYLAND, INDEPENDENCE,

AND THE

CONFEDERATION.

𝕱und-𝕻ublication, 𝕹o. 31.

MARYLAND, INDEPENDENCE,

AND THE

CONFEDERATION.

A Paper read before the Maryland Historical Society,

December 8th, 1890,

By WILLIAM J. HULL.

Baltimore, 1891.

PEABODY PUBLICATION FUND.

COMMITTEE ON PUBLICATION.

1891–92.

HENRY STOCKBRIDGE,
BRADLEY T. JOHNSON,
CLAYTON C. HALL.

PRINTED BY JOHN MURPHY & CO.
PRINTERS TO THE MARYLAND HISTORICAL SOCIETY.
BALTIMORE, 1891.

MARYLAND, INDEPENDENCE,

AND THE

CONFEDERATION.

THE three topics that occupied the most prominent place in the deliberations of the Continental Congress before the Declaration of
Independence, and the three that were of the most
vital importance to the colonies as a whole, were
those of political independence from the mother
country, of foreign alliances, and of armed resistance to the arbitrary measures enacted by the British Parliament and backed up by British arms.

A brief portrayal of Maryland's share in the
execution of these three great objects may serve a
useful purpose in enabling one the better to appre-
ciate Maryland's influence in the formation of the
Confederation and the Union.

I.

MARYLAND AND INDEPENDENCE.

In attempting to trace the continuity of history
it is not well, especially in so limited a paper as

this, to penetrate too far into the mists of antiquity; for the task of searching out the "first causes" of human conduct, as well as of the phenomena of nature, lies within the domain of speculative philosophy, and not of philosophic history. I shall, therefore, begin this relation of Maryland's influence upon American independence with an account of her attitude toward the first *immediate* cause of the Revolution—the Stamp Act of 1765.

In 1762, before the close of the French and Indian War, in consequence of the bold stand taken by the Maryland Assembly against the arbitrary demand of the proprietary, governor, minister, parliament, and general, to furnish supplies for the conduct of that war, the king expressed his stern displeasure at the "obstinate disobedience" of the Assembly of Maryland, and censured its members as not "animated by a sense of their duty to their king and country." This reproof was administered, Egremont wrote, "not to change their opinion," but "that they may not deceive themselves by supposing that their behavior is not seen here in its *true light.*" Thus when Maryland entered upon her energetic resistance to the Stamp Act, it was not the first time she had braved the British Lion and heard him growl; nor could she plead for her rebellious acts the immunity of a first offence. But when news reached the colony that the duties on stamped paper had been extended to America, there

was no hesitation as to the manner in which the
odious act should be received. Meetings were
held in every part of the province, and the people
expressed their detestation of the act and their
unalterable determination that it should never be
carried into effect, not only by bold and decided
resolutions against it, but also by acts of violence
against the persons and property of its supporters.
The freemen of Talbot county erected a gibbet
before the door of the court house, twenty feet
high, and hanged on it the effigy of a stamp
informer in chains, "in terrorem," until the Stamp
Act should be repealed ; and they resolved unanimously to hold in utter contempt and abhorrence
every stamp officer and every favorer of the Stamp
Act, and "to have no communication with any such,
not even to speak to him, unless to upbraid him
with his baseness." The effigy of Zachariah Hood,
the officer appointed for the distribution of the
stamps in Maryland, was paraded, whipped,
burned, hung, tarred and feathered, buried, and
treated with every sort of contumely in Baltimore,
Frederick, Annapolis, Elk Ridge, and other towns
of the province. Nor did this unhappy stamp dis-
tributor escape with mere punishment by proxy ;
his house at Annapolis was torn down, and he himself was forced to flee for protection from the irate
Maryland populace to General Gage in the city of
New York. But here also he felt the power of

American public opinion, now so thoroughly aroused; the Sons of Liberty of New York determined that, since " Mr. Hood had, by his flight, deprived his country of that justice it had a right to demand of him—the resignation of an office calculated to enslave them "—he should not evade that resignation while within their reach ; they accordingly forced him to resign his office and to promise never to undertake the duty again.

It was not by riotous measures alone that Maryland expressed her disapprobation of the tyrannical act. Daniel Dulany of Annapolis, confessedly the most distinguished lawyer America had produced, published a treatise entitled, "Considerations on the Propriety of Imposing Taxes on the British Colonies, for the purpose of Raising a Revenue, by Acts of Parliament." In this treatise Dulany proved conclusively the utter illegality of the Stamp Act, and by it he was at once placed in the foremost rank of the champions of the colonies in their struggle against taxes imposed upon them, without their consent, by the British Parliament. His prominence is shown by the fact that William Pitt, in Parliament, took honorable notice of his words, and adopted them as the ground-work of his own reasoning ; and his cogent arguments were undoubtedly of great influence in effecting the final repeal of the act whose illegality he so clearly proved.

He struck the key-note of the true Revolutionary spirit when he declared "that a garment of linsey-woolsey, when made the distinction of patriotism, is more honorable than the plumes and the diadem of an emperor without it. Let the manufacture of America be the symbol of dignity and the badge of virtue, and it will soon break the fetters of distress." However culpable may have been Dulany's reticence in the actual events of the Revolution, we may believe, with McMahon, that it was owing neither to opposition to the rights of America, nor to a servile submission to the views of the ministry; and "that, had he not been thrown into collision with the leaders of the war in Maryland, by the proclamation controversy, and thus involved in a discussion with them which excited high resentment on both sides, and kept him at a distance from them until the Revolution began, he would, most probably, have been found by their side, in support of the measures which led to it." (McMahon, I, 357.)

But opposition to the Stamp Act was not confined to individual writers and unofficial assemblies alone. One of the instructions given by the free-holders and freemen of Anne Arundel county to their delegates to the State Assembly "enjoined and required" them to use their "earnest endeavors,"— "I. That our essential inherent rights, and constitutional privileges, derived to us as British subjects, from the clear fountain of the British laws—

declared and confirmed to us by our charter—and the usages and customs of our province, be clearly and distinctly expressed and asserted by you in General Assembly. . . .

"II. That a committee be appointed early in the session by your House, and furnished with due instructions, to attend at the congress to be held at New York, the first day of next month [October 1, 1765], there to meet the commissioners from the other provinces on the continent, agreeable with the proposal in the Massachusetts circular letter, in order to confer on the circumstances of our country, and join in an humble and dutiful petition to his majesty for relief from the Stamp Act, with its numerous train of complicated evils ; and for redress of all our other grievances. . . ."

The first act of the General Assembly, when it was finally summoned by the governor, was to appoint three delegates to the congress to be held at New York, on the 7th of October, 1765, and to provide them with suitable instructions to present a petition to the king and British Parliament, praying "relief from the burdens and restraints lately laid upon the trade and commerce of the British colonies, and especially from the taxes imposed by the Stamp Act, whereby they are deprived, in some instances, of that invaluable privilege of Englishmen and British subjects—trials by juries ; and to take care that such representation should humbly

and decently, but expressly, contain an assertion of
the right of the colonists, to be exempt from all and
every taxations and impositions upon their persons
and property, to which they do not consent in a
legislative way, either by themselves or their rep-
resentatives freely chosen and appointed." The
three delegates appointed to this congress were
Colonel Edward Tilghman of Queen Anne's, William Murdock of Prince George's, and Thomas
Ringgold of Kent, who seem to have taken a prominent and useful part in the actions of that body;
'William Murdock was a member of the committee
that prepared an address to the king, and Col.
Tilghman of that which drafted the Memorial to
the House of Lords.

The Maryland Assembly in this same session
also promulgated a series of eight Declarations
"which," says Scharf, "from their dignified tone
and the unanimity with which they were adopted,
form one of the proudest pages of Maryland's history" (I. 538).

This same Assembly, in a later session, rebuked
the governor for his delay in convening them at a
period when they were desirous to unite with their
fellow citizens in the other colonies, in the preservation of their rights; refused to give him their
advice, as requested by him, concerning the disposal
of a cargo of stamped paper which was intended for
the colony—the members asserting that it was " not

agreeable to the sentiments of their constituents to give him any advice upon the subject;" and, on the day after the Stamp Act should have gone into effect (November 2, 1765), the Assembly appointed a "committee of grievances and courts of justice to inspect the form of the oaths of office, that have been, and now are usually taken by the several magistrates, and if the following clause be not inserted in the said oath," it was declared and resolved to be necessary, viz.: "To do equal law and right to all the king's subjects, rich and poor; and not to delay any person of common right, for the letters of the king, the Lord Proprietary, or of any other, or for any other cause; but if any such letters come to them, they shall proceed to do the law, the same letters notwithstanding." Truly, here is a declaration of legislative independence as distinct and emphatic as the far famed one of eleven years later!

In pursuance of this policy, so boldly announced, we find stated in the Maryland *Gazette* of December 10, 1765, that at "the last court in Frederick county, the magistrates taking into consideration the bad consequences that would attend a stop being put to the ordinary course of justice, if any notice was taken of the Stamp Act (which had never been legally transmitted to them), they, in a very full court, *unanimously resolved and ordered*, that all the business and process of that court should be transacted in the usual manner *without stamps*, and that such proceedings should be good and valid. The clerk of the court, apprehending damage to himself if he made any entry, or issued any process without stamped paper, refused to comply with the order of the court; upon which the court ordered him to be committed to prison for contempt. He then submitted, and was discharged, and proceeded on business as formerly."

Nor did the Marylanders stop here in proving to all concerned that they knew their rights, and that they meant to assert and maintain them in the most direct and effective manner possible. The Sons of Liberty of Baltimore and Anne Arundel counties, and the deputies of those of Kent, assembled on the 1st of March, 1766, at Annapolis, and made requisition upon the chief justice of the provincial court, the secretary of the province, the commissary general, and the judges of the land office, on pain of compulsion, to open their respective offices on the 31st of March, or earlier, if a majority of the supreme courts of the northern colonies should proceed in their business before that period. This requisition being peremptorily refused, the Sons assembled again on the day fixed by them, and insisted so emphatically upon their demand being granted that the provincial court yielded, and, after receiving a written indemnification for its action, passed the following order : " It is by the court here

2

ordered that the clerk of this court, from hence-
forth, issue all manner of process, file all pleadings,
give copies, and transact all business whatsoever,
in his office, for which application shall be made to
him by any inhabitant of this province, as usual,
without stamped paper." This order was at once
complied with by the clerk and other public officers,
and thus, one month and a half before the official
notification of the repeal of the Stamp Act was
received at Annapolis, the Marylanders had forced
the supreme court of their province to declare the
act absolutely *null and void.*

Hardly had the exultation over the repeal of the
Stamp Act subsided, when Parliament resorted to
a measure as arbitrary as, and still more odious to
the Americans than, the one just annulled; on June
29, 1767, a duty on various articles, including *tea,*
was imposed, which was to go into effect November
20, of the same year.

The Maryland Assembly, on hearing that such
an act was intended, declared, before their prorogation which shortly followed, that "life without liberty is worse than death," and took steps to preserve
that liberty from such an attack.[1]

The Assembly was not again convened until May
24, 1768, when it at once took into consideration the
circular letter of Massachusetts requesting the col-

[1] Namely, by taking up a collection to support an agent to represent them
in London.

onies to coöperate for the repeal of the late acts of
Parliament. Aware of the governor's instructions
to prorogue or dissolve them if they showed a disposition to receive this letter favorably, the House
prepared all their plans, and then replied to the
governor's message (that they should " treat the
letter with the contempt it deserved, by taking no
notice of it ") as follows : " We hope the conduct of
this house will ever evince their reverence and
respect for the laws, and faithful attachment to the
Constitution ; but we cannot be brought to resent
an exertion of the most undoubted constitutional
right of petitioning the Throne, or any endeavors
to procure and preserve an Union of the Colonies,
as an unjustifiable attempt to revive those distrac-
tions which it is said have operated so fatally to the
prejudice of both the colonies and the mother country. We have the warmest and most affectionate
attachment to our most gracious sovereign, and
shall ever pay the readiest and most respectful
regard to the *just* and *constitutional* power of the
British Parliament ; but we shall not be *intimidated*
by a few *sounding expressions* from doing what we
think is right." The next day the House sent a
reply to the Massachusetts circular, in which they
fully concurred in the opinion that the statutes
referred to " do infringe the great fundamental principle that no man can be taxed, but with his own
consent, given by himself, or his representative."

This reply caused their prompt prorogation, but not before they had promulgated a set of resolutions against the obnoxious measures, which for conclusiveness of argument and fearless assertion of rights will compare favorably with any other of the time.

Maryland also joined—June 20, 1769—with the other colonies in forming a strict non-importation agreement, and, in spite of wavering in other places, maintained it vigorously up to the breaking out of the war. She even administered a rebuke to Virginia for having fallen away from her non-importation agreement, passed resolutions to break off all commercial relations with New York, pursued the same course in regard to Rhode Island, for the same reason, and in a number of instances sent ships back to England, having refused to receive their cargoes.

The times were rife with disputes; no sooner had the Maryland Assembly expressed her defiance of England, than it became involved in a fierce contest with the proprietary governor over an attempt arbitrarily to extend his prerogative; the matters now at issue were an export duty on tobacco and the regulation of official salaries by proclamation. The contest was not confined to a war of words in the Houses of Assembly, for the press and people took the matter up and carried it on by means of essays, speeches, and " fistic " arguments, with the utmost spirit and, unfortunately, rancor. Charles Carroll of Carrollton first took a prominent part in public affairs at this time, and one of his declarations that " In a land of freedom this arbitrary exertion of prerogative will not, must not, be endured," became widely celebrated, and was used as the patriots' battle-cry of the early Revolution.

And now this battle-cry of freedom as well as all others, was to be in instant requisition : the Revolution, so long looming up threateningly in the political horizon, was about to materialize : and Maryland showed herself ready for the fray. When the act of the 10th of May, 1774, closed the port of Boston, Maryland promptly conveyed messages of sympathy and more practical means of support to the invested city. Baltimore resolved "That . . . the town of Boston is now suffering in the common cause of America, and that it is the duty of every colony in America to unite in the most effectual means to obtain" redress for her. And in a letter conveying this resolution, with a number of others, to Boston, Baltimore's Committee of Correspondence said : "Although the gentlemen of Philadelphia have recommended a general congress for proceeding by petition or remonstrance, we cannot see the least ground for expecting relief by it. The contempt with which a similar petition was treated in 1765, and many others since that period, convince us that policy or reasons of state, instead of justice and equity, are to prescribe the rule of our future conduct, and that something more sensible than supplications will best serve our purpose." It was probably at this time that Charles Carroll of Carrollton published his opinion of the status of affairs by exclaiming: "And do you think that our *pens* are to settle this mighty question? The *bayonet* must be the arbiter. The people *know* their rights—knowledge is resistance —and our only umpire is the God of battles!" Accordingly, the principal inhabitants set the example of arming themselves; and the delegates of the people, assembled in convention, besides levying and expending large sums of money for the procuring of ammunition, commanded every citizen to provide himself with arms, under pain of being proclaimed an enemy to his country. All this remarkable activity of martial preparation occurred many months before the actual outbreak of hostilities at the Battle of Lexington. Nor was Maryland making these preparations for herself alone: the Convention, on the 11th of December, 1774, " Resolved, unanimously, that if the late acts of Parliament, relative to the Massachusetts Bay, shall be attempted to be carried into execution by force in that colony, or if the assumed power of Parliament to tax the colonies shall be attempted to be carried into execution by force, in that or any other colony, that, in such case, this province will support such colony to the utmost of their power." John Adams in his "Novanglus," written in the latter part of 1774. pays this tribute to Maryland's efforts in the common cause; he says: " Maryland and the lower counties on the Delaware have already, to show all the world their approbation of the measures of New England, and their determination to join in them, with a generosity, and a wisdom and magnanimity which ought to make the Tories consider. taken the power of the militia into the hands of the people, without the governor or minister. and established it by their own authority, for the defence of Massachusetts as well as of themselves."

But Maryland did not content herself with promises of, and preparation for, future aid to her New England sister. Money was liberally subscribed in every county, and several vessels loaded with provisions were forwarded to Boston and Charlestown. In a Boston paper of August 29. 1774. we find the following notice: " Yesterday arrived at Marblehead. Capt. Perkins, from Baltimore. with 3000 bus. of Indian corn, 20 barrels of rye, and 21 barrels of bread, sent by the inhabitants of that place for the benefit of the poor of Boston, together with 1000 bus. of corn from Annapolis. sent in the same vessel, and for the same benevolent purpose."

Maryland thus emphatically countenanced the patriotic acts of Massachusetts, and thus gener-

ously supported her in the distress visited upon
her in consequence of those acts. But Maryland
herself was not barren of equally stirring and
patriotic events ; nor did Marylanders fall one iota
behind the men of Massachusetts in the boldness
and promptness of their resistance to English
tyranny. The fame of the " Boston Tea Party "
has become world-wide, and an account of it has
come to be considered essential to the completeness
of every text-book on American history ; while it
is hardly known, even to Maryland's own citizens,
that Annapolis was the scene of an event similar
to that of Boston, its peer in every respect, and in
several its superior. On the 15th of October, 1774,
only ten months after the tea was dumped into
Boston harbor, a vessel owned by Mr. Anthony
Stewart, of Annapolis, and loaded with tea con-
signed to an Annapolis firm, arrived at that port.
Mr. Stewart, influenced by his British sympathies,
paid the duty on the tea, preparatory to having it
landed ; this so incensed the patriots of Anne Arundel county that, after having compelled him to make
an humble apology, in a public meeting, for his
" act of the most pernicious tendency to the liberties of America," they obliged him to lend his
presence and assistance in destroying not only the
" detested plant " which formed the cargo, but the
vessel itself. The brig was run aground, near the
Windmill Point, the sails were set, the colors dis-

played, and amidst the acclamations of the multitude ship and cargo were burned to the water's edge. "In this deed," says Scharf, "there was no darkness, no disguise, no veil of secrecy, no shirking the responsibility, nor attempting to evade the risk of their actions. What was done was done deliberately, was done openly, in the face of day and in public meeting, under the very eyes of officials to whom probably every actor was personally known, and who would not fail to note them. Their rights had been contemned, their liberties invaded, their charter violated, and they determined to resist the wrong squarely and at once, be the consequences what they might." Nor was this the only burnt-offering offered up on the shrine of Liberty. Not long after this event, a ship owned by a merchant of Liverpool, and bound from that place to Baltimore with a cargo of salt, and other articles contrary to the non-importation association, ran aground on a shoal in the Chesapeake Bay near the mouth of West River, and she also was burned to the water's edge by the Maryland associators.

As Mr. Bancroft has shown, the *first* suggestion to hold a Continental Congress originated with the Sons of Liberty of New York; but the honor of first making this suggestion in a formal and effective manner, has been generally conceded to Virginia. Now, upon an examination of the facts, it will be seen that Maryland is entitled to an equal share of this honor. Although the Virginia House of Burgesses adopted a resolution, on the 27th of May, 1774, recommending their committee of correspondence to invite the other colonies to a general congress, this letter was not dated until the 31st of May; and on this same day the citizens of Baltimore adopted a similar resolution, and speak of it as if they were the originators of the movement. Moreover, the time and place (Philadelphia, September 20th, 1774,) of the meeting was fixed by the Maryland Convention, which with characteristic modesty, apologized to Virginia for preceding her in making this proposition, saying that she did so because " the limits of our province, and the number of its inhabitants, compared with yours, afforded an opportunity of collecting our general sense, before the sentiments of your colony could be regularly ascertained."

In the deliberations and acts of this ever memorable body, the Continental Congress, Maryland has every reason to be proud of the record made for her by her delegates. Samuel Chase, Charles Carroll of Carrollton, Thomas Johnson, and William Paca, are names that would grace the history of any age and land, and their efforts in the preservation of American liberties have cast bright lustre on their native State.

While fulfilling her part in the peaceful measures taken by Congress against British aggression,
Maryland proved that she was ready and willing
to resort to more warlike means. On April 29th,
1775, a day or two before the arrival of the news
from Lexington, on hearing that New York City
was to be fortified and garrisoned by the British,
the Maryland Convention gave their delegates in
Congress authority to " proceed even to the last ex-
tremity, if indispensably necessary for the safety
and preservation of their liberties and privileges."
The Convention which met at Annapolis on July
26th, 1775, seeing " no alternative but base submission or manly resistance," "approved the opposition by arms to the British troops."

And now we come to a discussion of the attitude
of Maryland toward the Declaration of Independence,—an attitude that has been characterized as the
outcome of jealousy, indifference, ruinous conservatism, and even cowardice. Of the latter charge, I
shall say nothing: the *facts* of Maryland's history
make *words* unnecessary. The charges of indifference and jealousy are also disproved by the same
cogent arguments,—the facts already related and
yet to be set forth. To conservatism Maryland
certainly pleads guilty, and it is her proud distinction that she was conservative at this important
epoch : but it was the best of all conservatism,—
what we know and admire now as ' progressive '

conservatism ; not slavish, nor sluggish, nor ruinous, but free and steady. and rational ; neither held back by fear of Britain's vengeance, nor precipitated by rash and foolish haste. Maryland has never, at any period of her history, had the slightest tincture of 'Sans-culottism,' in her make-up, and the debt of our country to the Chesapeake State for that element of 'progress united with conservatism,' at more than one national crisis, is perhaps greater than is commonly recognized.

At the beginning of the struggle, Maryland, in common with all the other colonies, was totally adverse to political independence from Great Britain ; and on more than one occasion she evinced her loyalty to the King by numerous resolves, addresses, and instructions to Congressional delegates. She was riveted to England by ties of kinship, religion, social relations, business interests, political policy, and, as she conceived, a strong sense of duty ; and ties such as these were not to be broken without the most careful deliberation, and without the most assured conviction that such a step would accord with the future welfare of the province as well as with present inclinations; and they were not broken until the short-sighted tyranny of the Mother Country forced upon the daughter the irresistible conclusion that it would best comport with her own and her people's prosperity for her to sever the maternal connection.

That this conclusion was finally reached by the
people of Maryland before it became too late, is
largely due to the efforts of Samuel Chase, the
"Demosthenes of Maryland," who is said to have
anticipated in Congress the regular proposition of
independence by a most impassioned and vehement
exclamation, that "By the God of Heaven, he owed
no allegiance to the King of Great Britain." Chase
left Congress in the early part of 1776, hastened to
Maryland, summoned county conventions in all the
counties, and assisted by Carroll, through speeches
and circular letters, convinced the people that the
time had come for expressing in words the independence which they had already virtually declared
in deeds. This conviction once thoroughly held, the
Marylanders acted with characteristic decision. A
new Convention was elected, which assembled on
the 21st of June, and, on the afternoon of the same
day that Moultrie so gallantly repulsed the British
fleet in its attack upon Charleston, at the very time
that Jefferson was reporting his draft of the Declaration to Congress (June 28, 1776), it empowered its
delegates "to concur with the other United Colonies, or a majority of them, in declaring the said
Colonies free and independent States."[1]

Five days later, on July 3d, while the Continental Congress was still considering the form of its

[1] John Adams writing to Chase, 7, 1, 1776: "Maryland behaved well;
Paca, generously and nobly."

declaration, the Convention directed the election of a new Convention, "to form a new government, by the authority of the people only;" and on the 6th of July, without waiting for the expected declaration of Congress, and before its final ratification could have been known, the Convention formally proclaimed the Independence of the Province of Maryland.

II.

Maryland and the Allies.

Having dwelt at some length on Maryland's share in making possible the Declaration of Independence, I shall now, much more briefly, outline her share in the successful maintenance of that independence; and shall commence with her influence in effecting foreign alliances.

It has impressed me as quite remarkable that there should have been such an intimate connection between the foreign allies of the Colonies and Maryland,—a relationship that was maintained throughout the Revolution, and has been continued in large degree to the present day. We find accounts in the Revolutionary records of banquets given by the citizens of Maryland to all the prominent foreigners in the American service, or of addresses presented to, and received from them. Lafayette, De Grasse, Rochambeau, De Kalb, Pulaski, Kosciusko, and

Paul Jones, were all associated in greater or less degree with Maryland and Maryland people. The relation between Lafayette and Baltimore was especially close: in a letter to Washington just before the Yorktown campaign, Lafayette says: "The State of Maryland have made to me every offer in their power. . . . The merchants of Baltimore have lent me a sum of about 2,000 pounds, which will procure some shirts, linen over-alls, and a few hats. The ladies will make up the shirts, and the over-alls will be made by the detachment, so that our soldiers have the chance of being a little more comfortable." . . . "My campaign began with a personal obligation to the inhabitants of Baltimore; at the end of it, I find myself bound to them by a new tie of everlasting gratitude."

Samuel Nicholson, of Chestertown, was Paul Jones's lieutenant in the battle between the Bon Homme Richard and Serapis. Count Pulaski was made a brigadier-general by Congress, in 1777, and granted permission to raise and command an independent corps: this corps he raised in Maryland, chiefly in Baltimore; and it was at the head of this corps through some of the bloodiest conflicts of the war, that the silken banner waved which is known to the world through the beautiful poem of Longfellow, and which is still to be seen in the rooms of the Maryland Historical Society. The military renown, won in America by Baron de Kalb, is inseparably joined with that of the Marylanders under his command; he was placed at the head of the Maryland Line not long after his arrival in this country, and retained this command until his heroic death at the Battle of Camden, in August, 1780.[1] It is said that De Kalb's dying moments were spent in expressing his praise of the noble Maryland regiment, and his admiration of Gist, and its other gallant officers.

But not only was Maryland closely connected with our foreign allies after their appearance on the stage of the Revolution, but she was also influential in causing these actors to appear. In order to identify Canada with the cause of the American Colonies, or to procure her neutrality at the least, Congress on February 15, 1776. " Resolved, That a committee of three (two of whom to be members of Congress) be appointed to repair to Canada, there . . . to assure them, that it is our earnest desire to adopt them into our union, as a sister colony, . . . and to urge the necessity the people are under of immediately taking some decisive step, to put themselves under the protection of the United Colonies." Of the three commissioners appointed on this dangerous and delicate mission, two, Samuel Chase and

[1] October 14, 1780, Congress passed a resolution for the erection of a monument to the memory of De Kalb in the city of Annapolis, and at a recent day it has been placed by the side of the State House in the "Ancient City" in the form of a statue of the hero; more a credit to the gratitude of the American people than to the genius of the artist.

Charles Carroll of Carrollton, were Marylanders; and it was also "Resolved, That Mr. Carroll be requested to prevail on Mr. John Carroll (also a Marylander, and the first archbishop in America) to accompany the committee to Canada, to assist them in such matters as they shall think useful." This mission was unsuccessful, in so far as the active coöperation of Canada was concerned, but this was due, not to the incapacity of the commissioners, but to the defeat of Montgomery's army, the contributions levied on the inhabitants, the invincible opposition of the priests, and more especially, to the inconsistency of the two addresses of Congress: the one to the Canadians declaring "that we hold sacred the rights of conscience, and you may promise to the whole people, solemnly in our name, the free and undisturbed exercise of their religion; and, to the clergy, the full, perfect, and peaceable possession and enjoyment of all their estates; that the government of every thing relating to their religion and clergy, shall be left entirely in the hands of the good people of that province, &c., &c.;"[1] while the other to the People of Great Britain, declares, alluding to the "Quebec Act" passed by Parliament, "That we think the legislature of Great Britain is not authorized, by the constitution, to establish a religion, fraught with sanguinary and impious tenets . . . . in any quarter of the globe." . . . . "Nor

[1] Journals, March 20, 1776.

5

can we suppress our astonishment that a British Parliament should ever consent to establish in that country (Canada), a religion that has deluged your island in blood, and dispersed impiety, bigotry, persecution, murder and rebellion through every part of the world."[1]

Although the Journals of the Continental Congress are entirely silent on the subject of European alliance before the latter part of 1776, we know from a letter of John Adams to Dr. Rush, dated 30th September, 1805, that the first move in this direction was made by a Maryland man. In this letter John Adams says: " Samuel Chase made a motion in Congress in the fall of 1775 to send ambassadors to France. John Adams seconded the motion. You know the state of the nerves of Congress at that time. . . . . Whether the effect of the motion resembled the shock of electricity, of mesmerism, or of galvanism, the most exactly, I leave you philosophers to determine ; but the grimaces, the agitations, and convulsions were very great." Some idea of the commotion caused in Congress by Chase's proposal may be seen in a speech made on that occasion by the Rev. Dr. Zubly of Georgia (October 6, 1775) ; in the course of this speech, Dr. Zubly said : " There are persons in America who wish to break off with Great Britain. A proposition has been made to apply to France and Spain ;

[1] Journals, October 21, 1774.

before I agree to it I apprehend the man who should propose it would be torn to pieces like De Witt." Chase replied to this speech by declaring that there was amongst them on the floor of Congress a Judas Iscariot in the person of J. J. Zubly of Georgia ; and he produced such ample proofs of his assertion, that Zubly precipitately left Congress, and soon went over to the enemy.

Having spoken of the part he took in the debate following this motion, Mr. Adams (in the same letter) continues : " After all our argumentation, however, we could not carry our motion ; but, after twenty subtle projects to get rid of it, the whole terminated in a committee of secret correspondence."

This Committee of Secret Correspondence was appointed November 29, 1775, and was composed of Harrison, Franklin, Johnson, Dickinson and Jay. " The sole purpose for which the committee was appointed," says the Secret Journals (Vol. II., Foreign Relations), was to "correspond with our friends in Great Britain, Ireland, and *other parts of the world.*" Authority was given to them to employ and send out agents on the service. It is noticeable that none of the New England delegates were appointed on this committee (although Hancock was President of Congress at the time),— probably because, by their support of radical measures, they had made themselves obnoxious to the more conservative party in Congress; this reason may be assigned, with equal probability, as an explanation of Samuel Chase's absence from this important committee. Of Chase's prominence in the movement towards foreign alliances there can be no doubt. As we have seen, John Adams gives to him the credit of first introducing the question before Congress. A few months later, on hearing that the plan of confederation and foreign alliance still met with opposition and delay, he hastened back to Philadelphia to again lend his support to the effecting of these two important objects. The anxiety of his mind lest they should not be carried through is plainly to be seen in a letter which he wrote to Richard Henry Lee at this time: ". . . . I hurried to Congress to give my little assistance to the framing a confederation and a plan for foreign alliance,—both of them subjects of the greatest importance, and which, in my judgment, demand the greatest despatch. . . . . The whole might, in my opinion, be settled, if candour, justice, and the real interests of America were attended to. We do not all see the importance, nay, the *necessity* of a confederacy. We shall remain weak, distracted and divided in our councils; our strength will decrease; we shall be open to all the arts of the insidious court of Britain, and no foreign court will attend to our applications for assistance, before we are confederated. What contract will a foreign state make with us when we cannot agree among ourselves?"

In spite of secret treason and determined opposition to the plan of a foreign alliance, Chase and his supporters finally carried the day, the Secret Committee of Correspondence was appointed (November 29, 1775), and, as a result of their labors, that Treaty with France was secured, without which the Revolution would hardly have succeeded. Although the Treaty was made at the time when Maryland was vigorously maintaining the claims of the Colonies as a whole to the unsettled Western lands, and was persistently refusing to accede to the Confederation until those claims should be recognized, the Maryland Assembly unanimously approved the French alliance as equal, honorable and wise, and pledged themselves and the State of Maryland to be bound by the provisions of the Treaty and faithfully to fulfil them as good and true allies.

In the hour of American triumph, Maryland did not forget America's debt of gratitude to France. When the British General and Admiral in May, 1782, informed Washington that they were authorized to negotiate a treaty of peace, the Assembly of Maryland, to show their appreciation of the services rendered by the French allies, "Resolved, unanimously, That it is the opinion of this State that peace with Great Britain and all the world is an object truly desirable, but that war with all its calamities is to be preferred to national dishonor. That it is the sentiment of this State that any negotiation for peace or truce, not agreeable to the Alliance with France, is inadmissible ; that every danger ought to be encountered, every event hazarded, rather than sully our national character, or violate, in the least degree, our connection with our great and good ally, and that good faith, gratitude and safety forbid any treaty for peace or truce with Great Britain, but in conjunction with France, or with her consent first obtained."

III.

MARYLAND IN THE ARMY.

The military record of Maryland both on sea and land during the Revolution, is one of which every Marylander should be proud, and upon which he may be pardoned for dilating whenever a suitable opportunity presents itself. The scope of this paper hardly offers such opportunity, but I cannot refrain from outlining the main features of that record.

In the first place, a Maryland man, Thomas Johnson, first governor of the State, gave to the American army its commander-in-chief, George Washington. Virginia claims Washington as a native-born citizen; Massachusetts claims that she gave him to Virginia; but the indisputable fact remains that on the 15th of June, 1775, Thomas Johnson, of Maryland, nominated him as commander-in-chief of the Continental army, and that he was upon that nomination unanimously elected to the position. The contemporary accounts of this event are lamentably scarce and superficial. Tradition has preserved, and current histories have repeated, accounts of how the ' Virginians were in favor of Washington's election before he was nominated,' and how ' John Adams met Samuel Adams outside of the Congress hall on the very day of the nomination and told him that Washington was the man for the place;' but the fact that he was actually nominated and supported by a Marylander has been utterly neglected. On the face of it, this mere nomination seems a sufficiently unimportant service. But when we consider that Washington had not then attained the all engrossing position that he afterwards came to fill in the eyes of the world, that his merits were then comparatively untried, and his name but little known, and then view his nomination through the medium of the inestimable services he afterwards rendered to his country, this service takes on a new aspect, and assumes greatly increased proportions; so that candor compels us to acknowledge that it was, in reality a service eminently influential in the final success of the American cause.[1]

John Adams refers to Thomas Johnson as the nominator of Washington to the position of commander-in-chief, placing his name and this service in connection with the greatest names and services of the Revolution ; viz., with those of Washington and the command of the army, Jefferson and the Declaration, Richard Henry Lee and the Resolutions of June 7, Samuel Chase and the motion for foreign relations.[2]

Maryland, having chosen the general, did not desert him, but, from Boston to Yorktown remained his constant friend and supporter, sharing in his victories, and doing much toward sustaining his reverses. In his darkest hours, when New York and Philadelphia were in the hands of the British, before the alliance with France, when the army was famishing and freezing in the camp at Valley Forge, and when the Conway Cabal was formed by officers in the army and countenanced by members of Congress to displace him and substitute Gates, it was Maryland who rallied to the General's support both in Congress halls and on battle fields.

Charles Carroll of Carrollton, was one of the warmest friends and advocates of Washington on

[1] Gist saved Washington's life.
[2] Letter to Timothy Pickering, August 6, 1822, and see Letter to Richard H. Lee. Works of John Adams, Vol. X, page 396.

the Congressional Committee which vindicated him
from the charges made by the Conway Cabal.

Food and clothing were sent from Maryland
farms and homes to the soldiers at Valley Forge.
Mrs. Margaret Jane Ramsay, wife of the gallant
colonel, followed the army from place to place, attended by a servant, carrying a chest of medicine,
soothing the last moments of soldiers dying on the
field of battle, and alleviating the soldiers' sufferings
in the small-pox stricken tents of Valley Forge.
General Smallwood was sent by Congress to Maryland to encourage and hasten the raising of new
levies,—a task in which he was eminently successful. Johnson left Congress, hastened to Maryland,
raised a small army, and with it joined Washington's troops. And Chase, on behalf of Congress,
published a powerful address to the people of
America to counteract the insidious conciliatory
bills of the British Parliamentary Commissioners,
which were being diligently circulated by the Tories.

Maryland was one of the free States to whom
Congress made its first appeal for soldiers (June
14, 1775), and one of the Maryland companies
raised in response to this appeal was the first from
the south to reach Cambridge, the seat of war (August, 1775) at that time. Nor was it only on this
first occasion that Maryland showed her promptness and willingness in supplying men and provisions for the common defence; throughout the war

she came liberally and readily to the front in sacrificing the lives and money of her citizens, and, without intending any "odious comparison" in the statement, General Smallwood, in a letter to the Maryland Council of Safety (October, 1776), testifies " that none of the States have filled their quotas of troops but Maryland." And the troops she furnished, proved themselves of the right stuff. They were confessedly the favorites of Washington ; and the heroes of his first campaign. At the battle of Long Island, when Sullivan's troops had been routed, and when the rest of the American army was in most imminent danger of being surrounded and cut off. General Stirling determined upon a sacrifice of a part of his army for the safe retreat of the rest ; selecting a band of less than four hundred Marylanders, he succeeded in keeping at bay a force of five times his number, and thus saved the army. Says Mr. Thomas W. Field, in his " Battle of Long Island " : " The sacrifice of their lives, so freely made by the generous and noble sons of Maryland, had not been made in vain. An hour, more precious to American liberty than any other in its history, had been gained ; and the retreat of many hundreds of their countrymen had been secured across the dreadful creek and marsh whose treacherous tide and slime now covered so many of their brave comrades."

The gallantry displayed by the Marylanders in the actions at Kip's Bay and Harlem Heights, was warmly praised by Washington in his letters to Congress.

At the Battle of White Plains, when the rest of the brigade to which they were attached had retreated, Colonel Smallwood's regiment sustained the heavy fire of artillery and musketry that was centred upon them, for full half an hour while the brigade was making good its retreat.

Colonel Moses Rawlings and his Marylanders were the heroes of Fort Washington.

The gallant defence of Fort Mifflin was made by Colonel Samuel Smith of Baltimore, and his Maryland artillerymen ; in a letter to Congress (17 November, 1777) informing them of the fall of this fort, Washington says : " I am sorry to inform you that Fort Mifflin was evacuated the night before last, after a defence which does credit to the American arms, and will ever reflect the highest honor upon the officers and men of the garrison. The works were entirely beat down ; every piece of cannon dismounted, and one of the enemy's ships so near that she threw grenades into the fort and killed men upon the platforms, from her tops, before they quitted the Island."[1] As a reward for his conduct on this occasion, Colonel Smith was presented with a sword by Congress.

[1] Sparks, V, p. 151.

It is related that, at the Battle of Monmouth,[1] when General Lee, commanding the advanced corps, was making his treacherous retreat upon the rear division, thus placing the whole army in imminent danger of falling into confusion, and the enemy were within a few minutes' march, Washington called for an officer to check the British advance: Colonel Nathaniel Ramsay, of Baltimore, promptly presented himself, and the commander-in-chief, taking him by the hand, thus addressed him: "If you can stop the British ten minutes, till I form, you will save my army!" Colonel Ramsay answering, "I will stop them or fall!" proved as good as his word, and succeeded in keeping the enemy in check for half an hour, until the main division under Patterson and Smallwood formed, and saved the day.

One of the two divisions with which General Wayne effected the memorable capture of Stony Point, was led by Major John Stewart, of Maryland,[2] and composed mostly of soldiers of the Maryland Line.

It was almost entirely through the efforts of the Maryland companies under his command,[3] that Major Henry Lee succeeded in capturing another strong British fort on Paulus Hook.

[1] Cf. "Colonel Nathaniel Ramsay,"—a monograph published by the Maryland Historical Society. Fund Publication, No. 24.

[2] Congress awarded a Medal to Major Stewart for his gallantry on this occasion.

[3] See Major Lee's Report to Congress, for an account of the conduct of the other companies.

This brilliant episode closed the military career of Maryland in the North : a career adorned throughout by the utmost bravery, endeared through many an inestimable service, graced by many a triumph, hallowed by many a noble death, and unspotted by a single blemish Nor did Maryland's " Northern laurels turn." like those of Gates, "to Southern willows." but blossomed rather into Southern immortelles.

On the disastrous field of Camden, when all the rest of the army had made a shameful retreat, the two Maryland brigades and the Delaware battalion were left alone to sustain the onslaught of the entire British army, and to share the glorious death of their leader, the gallant Baron de Kalb. Six hundred of the eight hundred Marylanders engaged were left dead upon the field.

The Battle of Cowpens was sustained and won by the " Lion-hearted Howard " and his Maryland regiment. At the close of the day, Colonel Howard is said to have held the swords of seven British officers whom he had taken prisoners. including that of General O'Hara. who had clung to his stirrups asking quarter. [1]

The memorable retreat of Greene from the Catawba to the Dan was protected by a picked body of Maryland and Virginia soldiers under the command of Colonel Otho H. Williams. It is generally

[1] Harper's Magazine, LXV, 23.

42

admitted that the success of this achievement was due largely to the masterly manœuvres of the covering party.

At the Battle of Guilford, when the Virginia and North Carolina militia had been routed, the First Maryland regiment under Colonels Gunby and Howard, came to the rescue, and succeeded in winning a remarkable victory. Says Judge Johnson in his " Life of Greene" (II, 15), speaking of this battle: " Excepting the infantry of the legion[1] and Kirkwood's little corps of Delaware, the first regiment of the Marylanders was the only body of men in the American army who could be compared to the enemy in discipline and experience; and it is with confidence that we challenge the modern world to produce an instance of better service performed by the same number of men in the same time. They did not exceed two hundred and eighty-five in number. Yet, unassisted they drove from the field in the first instance, the thirty-third regiment, three hundred and twenty-two strong, supported by the Jägers and light infantry of the Guards. Before they had yet breathed from the performance of this service, they pierced the flank of the first battalion of the Guards, and aided by the cavalry of Washington, dissipated a corps far exceeding their own in number, and the very boast of the British nation. Valleys of grape-shot poured

[1] The legion was composed largely of Maryland troops.

through their own ranks by the enemy, and the near approach of two British regiments on their left flank, arrested them in the pursuit; but they calmly, and in perfect order, returned to their position and exhibited a spirit that seemed only to covet more arduous service.

The charge of the Maryland Line at the Battle of Eutaw is too well known and celebrated to need commendation here.[1] It was on that occasion that General Greene observes, speaking of the Maryland corps: "I am at a loss which most to admire, the gallantry of the officers or the good conduct of the men. . . . The uncommon intrepidity of Colonel Williams . . . . exceeded anything I ever saw . . . . Colonel Howard is as good an officer as the world affords, and deserves a statue of gold, no less than the Roman and Grecian heroes.[2]" The thanks of Congress were presented[3] "to the officers and men of the Maryland and Virginia brigades, and Delaware battalion of Continental troops, for the unparalleled bravery and heroism by them displayed, in advancing to the enemy through an incessant fire, and charging them with an impetuosity and ardor that could not be resisted."

The troops of Maryland under Gist did good service in the field and trenches of Yorktown, and the executive and State government, generously

[1] Letter 9–12–81.
[2] Caldwell, Life of Greene, 175.
[3] 29 October, 1781.

sustained by the people, were so active in furnishing the combined armies with supplies necessary to sustain the siege, as to call forth from Washington the warmest praise and thanks.

It is somewhat remarkable that the news of the two greatest successes gained by the Americans during the war, namely the capitulation of Burgoyne and of Cornwallis, should have been carried to Congress and so to the country at large, by Maryland men. The news of Burgoyne's surrender was conveyed to Congress by Major Wilkinson, afterwards General Wilkinson of Maryland; the joy occasioned by the receipt of these glad tidings may be better imagined than described, considering that they came at a time when the affairs of State were at the darkest, and told of the first great American victory, the turning-point in the War for Independence.

The news that "Cornwallis is taken" was carried with remarkable speed to Congress by Colonel Tench Tilghman, Washington's private secretary, also a Maryland man;[1] a horse properly caparisoned, and an elegant sword, were presented by Congress to the bearer of these great tidings,— tidings of an event that virtually ended the War for Independence, and it ranks in historic interest with the famous Ride of Paul Revere, the Ride in

---

[1] Washington says of Tilghman: "He has been in every action in which the main army was concerned, and has been a faithful assistant to me for five years, a great part of which time he refused to receive pay."

which the Good News was brought from Aix to Ghent, Sheridan's Ride, and Putnam's Ride at Horse Neck.

Judge Johnson in his life of Greene (II, p. 345), gives to Captain Wilmot, of Maryland, the credit of being the last American to die in his country's cause in the Revolutionary War; on the 14th of November, 1782, Wilmot, in conjunction with Kosciusko, planned and carried into effect an expedition against a party of the enemy's wood-cutters, on James Island, and in it he lost his life.

It was in Maryland, in the Senate Chamber at Annapolis, that the last scene in the drama of the Revolution was enacted,[1]—the surrender by General Washington, to the civil authorities, of that sword with which, under God, he had achieved the independence of his country; an event justly characterized as one of the most memorable and extraordinary recorded in the history of the world, and one which has cast a bright lustre of historic interest upon the capital of our State.

IV.

MARYLAND AND THE CONFEDERATION.

On the twenty-eighth of June, 1776, Samuel Chase, who has been called " the torch that lighted up the Revolutionary flame in Maryland," hurrying

[1] December 23, 1783.

from the Maryland House of Delegates in which had just been passed the decree that severed the political bonds uniting the colony to Great Britain, sent the following dispatch to John Adams, then laboring for independence in the halls of Congress: "I am this moment from the House to procure an express to follow up the post, with a unanimous vote of our Convention for independence. See the glorious effects of county instructions. Our people have fire if not smothered . . . *Now for a government!*" This last sentiment was an echo of that which prevailed at the moment in the Maryland Assembly: for in the very Act of dissolving their allegiance to the British Crown, the Assembly made provision for the establishment of a general government which should confirm and perpetuate the rights assumed by their Declaration of Independence.

By this memorable Resolution, the Maryland delegates in Congress were "empowered to concur with the other United Colonies, or a majority of them in . . . forming such further compact and confederation between them . . . . as shall be adjudged necessary for securing the liberties of America; and this Colony will hold itself bound by the resolutions of a majority of the United Colonies in the premises: provided, the sole and exclusive right of regulating the internal government and police of this colony be reserved to the people thereof."

The task before the new nation was full of danger that threatened disaster, and of problems that seemed to many impossible of solution. In the concise words of James Madison,[1] it consisted in the establishment of a "system (of government) founded on popular rights, and so combining a federal form with the forms of individual republics, as may enable each to supply the defects of the other and obtain the advantage of both." And such a system was to be formed between thirteen states, differing in extent, wealth and population, as well as in habits, education, and religious opinions, and between some of which disputes existed relative to boundaries, imposts, and other matters. Viewed through the medium of subsequent events in our history, the gravity and importance of the situation is apparent. But, however justly "reluctant" the people were to undertake the task, their " necessities " were undoubtedly " grinding." The same vital considerations that urged a union of the Colonies, dictated a union of the States. In the darkest hours of the Revolution, surrounded by the clouds of defeat and treason, as yet unaided by any foreign power, threatened with the dire vengeance and pursued by the remorseless energy of an infuriated King, the people as a whole fully concurred

[1] Elliot, V, 109.

with the sentiment expressed by Franklin, that
" they must all hang together, or they would as-
suredly all hang separately." And on the other
hand, it appeared but too probable that the contend-
ing passions and ambitions of separate governments,
the mutual jealousies and discordant interests of so
many rival powers, would inevitably expose them
to a renewal of those scenes of violence which
had laid waste the fertile plains of Europe, and
drenched them with the blood of countless millions.

Goaded on by circumstances threatening such
perils, and led by hopes of "common defence,
security of liberties, and mutual and general welfare." the question of a general government was
early broached. As far back as July 21. 1775,
Congress having " resolved itself into a committee
of the whole to take into consideration the state of
America. Dr. B. Franklin submitted to their consideration " thirteen proposed articles of confederation. Thomas Jefferson,[1] alluding to this proposed
plan of union, says : " I approved it highly. He
(Dr. Franklin) showed it to others. Some thought
as I did ; others were revolted at it. We found it
could not be passed, and the proposing it to Congress as the subject for any vote whatever would
startle many members so much, that they would
suspect we had lost sight of reconciliation with
Great Britain, and that we should lose much more

[1] Jefferson's "Works," IX, p. 303.

ground than we should gain by the proposition. Yet, that the idea of a more firm bond of union than the undefined one under which we then acted might be suggested and permitted to grow, Dr. Franklin informed Congress that he had sketched the outlines of an instrument which might become necessary at a future day, if the minority continued pertinacious; and would ask leave for it to lay on the table of Congress, that the members might in the meantime be turning the subject in their minds, and have something more perfect prepared by the time it should become necessary. This was agreed to by the timid members, only on condition that no entry whatever should be made in the journals of Congress relative to this instrument. . . . . . "

The concluding paragraph of these articles is noteworthy for the advanced stage that the mind of Franklin had already attained toward independence.[1] It provided that "the union thereby established is to continue firm, till the terms of reconciliation proposed in the petition of the last Congress to the king are agreed to; till the acts since made, restraining the American commerce and fisheries, are repealed; till reparation is made for the injury done to Boston, by shutting up its port, for the burning of Charlestown, and for the expense of this unjust war; and till all the British troops are withdrawn from America. On the arrival of these

[1] See Secret Journals, Vol. 1, p. 288.

events, the colonies will return to their former connexion and friendship with Britain; but on failure thereof, this confederation is to be perpetual."

But the times were not yet ripe for so decisive a step. The subject was not brought before Congress again until June 7, 1776, when the famous twin resolutions of Richard Henry Lee were offered, one of which provided "That a plan of Confederation be prepared and transmitted to the respective Colonies for their consideration and approbation."

On June 11, 1776, it was " Resolved, That a committee be appointed to prepare and digest the form of a confederation to be entered into between these colonies;" and on the following day, it was " Resolved, That the committee to prepare and digest the form of confederation to be entered into between these colonies, consist of a member from each colony." Maryland's representative on this committee was Thomas Stone.

It was not until Friday, the twelfth of July, 1776, that this committee reported a draft of the proposed confederation, consisting of twenty articles. After taking stringent measures for the prevention of the circulation outside of Congress of any information concerning the proposed articles, Congress, on Monday, the twenty-second of the same month, resolved itself into a committee of the whole to take the report into consideration. The debate in committee was continued from day to day until Tuesday, the twentieth of August, when the amended form was reported back to the House. It was now laid aside until the eighth of April, 1777, when the Articles were again taken up, and discussed and postponed from day to day and month to month until November 15, 1777, at which time, having been reduced to Thirteen, they were finally adopted.

In the long debate in the committee of the whole, from July 22 to August 20, Maryland's delegates, Samuel Chase in particular, were prominent and influential. It was early in this debate that Maryland entered upon the far-sighted policy by which she was determined to shape her own course in her relations with her sister States, and which was in the end to have such a vital influence upon the establishment and development of the Union itself. It was soon found that a wide diversity of sentiment prevailed among the States on three important points: First, as to the mode of *voting* in Congress,—whether by States, or according to wealth or population; second, as to the rule by which the *expenses* of the union should be *apportioned* among the States; third, relative to the disposition of the vacant and unpatented western lands.

In the discussion on the first of these questions, the grasping policy of some States was first mani-

fested.[1] The Virginia delegates in particular intro-
duced three propositions, each having for its object
the aggrandizement of the large States in presence
of the ballot-box at the expense of the small. The
discussion waxed hot, when Samuel Chase, doubt-
less hoping to throw oil upon the troubled waters,
came forward in the following speech: "He observed that this article was the one most likely to
divide us of any one proposed in the draught then
under consideration: that the larger colonies had
threatened they would not confederate at all, if their
weight in Congress should not be equal to the
numbers of the people they added to the confederacy; while the smaller ones declared against a
union, if they did not retain an equal vote for the
protection of their rights. That it was of the utmost consequence to bring the parties together, as,
should we sever from each other, either no foreign
power will ally with us at all, or the different
States will form different alliances, and thus in-
crease the horrors of those scenes of civil war and
bloodshed, which in such a state of separation and
independence, would render us a miserable people.
That our importance, our interests, our peace required that we should confederate, and that mutual sacrifices should be made to effect a compro-
mise of this difficult question. I am of opinion
that the smaller colonies will lose their rights, if

[1] See Secret Journals, I, p. 317 ff.

they are not in *some* instances allowed an equal
vote; and that therefore, a discrimination should
take place among the questions which should come
before Congress. That the smaller States should
be secured in all questions concerning life or liberty, and the greater ones, in all respecting property. I therefore propose that in votes relating to
money, the voice of each colony shall be propor-
tioned to the number of its inhabitants."[1] This
proposal failed of its object, however, and the discussion waxed hotter and hotter.[2] "Great heats,
much ill humor, and intemperate declarations
were produced from some members. Dr. Franklin at length brought the debate to a close with one
of his little apologues. He observed 'that at the
time of the union of England and Scotland, the
Duke of Argyle was most violently opposed to that
measure, and among other things predicted that,
as the whale had swallowed Jonah, so Scotland
would be swallowed by England. However,' said
the Doctor, 'when Lord Bute came into the government, he soon brought into its administration so
many of his countrymen, that it was found in event
that Jonah had swallowed the whale.' This little
story produced a general laugh and restored good
humor," and the Article giving each State one vote
was finally adopted.

[1] See Jefferson's "Works," I, p. 30.
[2] See Jefferson's "Works," VIII, 499; I, 31–32.

8

With respect to the expenses of the union, it was
proposed that they should be paid by the States in
proportion to the number of inhabitants of every
age, sex, and quality (except Indians not paying
taxes) in each State, the number to be taken every
three years.[1] In the debate in the committee on
this proposition, Chase moved to insert the word
"white" before "inhabitants," and supported his
motion in a strong speech, arguing that *slaves* were
property and should not be counted as people.
Chase was ably answered by John Adams, his
amendment was defeated, and the Article was
reported to Congress in the form originally proposed. But when the question came to be discussed
in Congress, determined resistance was again offered
to the counting of slaves as people and to the apportionment of taxes on that basis, and two propositions were made,—one, that such apportionment
be based upon the value of all property, except
household goods and wearing apparel, within each
State; the other, that the value of all land within
each State, granted to or surveyed for any person,
together with the buildings and improvements
thereon, be the basis of taxation. This latter
proposition was "passed in the affirmative," and
embodied as Article VIII in the final draft. Owing
to the meagreness of available records, it is impossible to say certainly who offered this proposition,

[1] See Jefferson's "Works," I, p. 27; Adams' "Works," II, p. 496.

and who supported it in debate; but from the few recorded speeches in the committee of the whole, I am inclined to credit its proposal to Dr. Witherspoon, of New Jersey.[1] That State, and all those south of Pennsylvania voted unanimously in its favor (5), against the four northern states, and two (New York and Pennsylvania) divided.

In Maryland's subsequent objections to the Confederation, it was proposed that after the words "granted to or surveyed for" in this Article, there be inserted the words "or which shall hereafter be granted to or surveyed for any person." This proposal was defeated by a vote of eight to four; but in it we see an evidence of Maryland's determined and eventually successful stand that the vast vacant territories claimed by a few States should, in some way or another, be made to benefit the United States as a whole.

And this leads us to a consideration of the third chief point of difficulty in the adoption of the Confederation,—the question as to the disposition of the vacant and unpatented western lands.

In the first draft of the Confederation occurred the following Article (XIV): "No purchases of land hereafter to be made of the Indians by colonies or private persons, before the limits of the colonies are ascertained, to be valid. All purchases of lands not included within those limits, where

[1] See Jefferson's "Works," 1, p. 30.

ascertained, to be made by contracts between the
United States assembled, or by persons for that
purpose authorized by them, and the great councils
of the Indians, *for the general benefit of all the United
Colonies.*" In the discussion over this Article in the
committee of the whole, as far back as July 25, 1776,
Samuel Chase made a strong fight to have it stand,
but the committee refused to report it, and it was
accordingly stricken out. Here is apparently the
first suggestion that a union of the colonies should
be based upon a territorial commonwealth,—a suggestion originating with and supported by a dele-
gate from Maryland. But more than the suggestion
of such a union is to be ascribed to Maryland ; the
brunt of the battle for its accomplishment fell upon
her. For five years she strove to realize her ideal,
and her efforts were eventually crowned with success. Arguing from the just principle " That in
order to render the present union and confederacy
firm and perpetual, it is essential that the limits of
each respective territorial jurisdiction be ascertained
by the articles of confederation," the Maryland delegates made four unsuccessful endeavors to vest in
Congress the right " to fix the western boundaries
of such States as claim to the South Sea, and to
dispose of all land beyond the boundaries so ascertained for the benefit of the United States." These
efforts were made for a long time unsupported by
the delegates of any other State ; and it was only in

the absence of the Maryland delegates that Congress added the clause to the Ninth Article, which provided that no State should be deprived of territory for the benefit of the United States.

The further steps in Maryland's struggle for the nationalization of the western lands have been so thoroughly treated by Professor H. B. Adams, in a monograph published by the Maryland Historical Society, that I shall dwell no longer upon the subject than to borrow from the work referred to, a sentence summing up the true significance of Maryland's attitude at this momentous epoch in American history. Says Professor Adams: "The credit of suggesting and successfully urging in Congress, that policy which has made this country a great national commonwealth, composed of "free, convenient, and independent governments," bound together by ties of permanent territorial interests, the credit of originating this policy belongs to Maryland, and to her alone."[1]

In the objections made by the Maryland Assembly to the Confederation, June 22, 1778, were advocated two great American principles, which in view of present political discussion, are worthy of mention; these are manhood citizenship as opposed to property qualifications, and protection to home labor as opposed to unrestricted immigration.

[1] Fund Publication No. XI. "Maryland's Influence in founding a National Commonwealth," p. 30.

In Article IV, the Maryland delegates moved to strike out the restriction upon the right of *paupers* to all privileges and immunities of free citizens in the several States; and they endeavored, also, to fix the maintenance of poor immigrants from one State to another, upon the State whence they emigrated.

These two endeavors, together with Maryland's chief mission regarding the western lands, were unsuccessful at the time, and so Maryland steadily refused to ratify the Confederation. Finally Congress decided that it was "more advisable to press upon those States which could remove the embarrassments respecting the western country, a liberal surrender of a portion of their territorial claims." An appeal to that effect was accordingly sent by Congress to the claimant States, which, following the example of New York, authorized their delegates to surrender the major part of their claims to the western country. For so doing, these States deserve credit, perhaps, not for being generous, but for not persisting in claims more or less unwarranted, at a critical period in the Revolution.

So much being accomplished, Maryland—"from an earnest desire to conciliate the affection of the sister States, to convince all the world of our unalterable resolution to support the independence of the United States and the alliance with his Most Christian Majesty, and to destroy forever any apprehension of our friends, or hope in our ene-

mies, of this State being again united to Great
Britain "—yielded her objections to the Confederation, and empowered her delegates to subscribe the
Articles (February 2, 1781). But, true to the policy
which they conceived to be to the interest not only
of their own constituents but also of the whole
Confederation, the Maryland Assembly in their
authorizing Act "declared, that by acceding to the
said Confederation, this State does not relinquish,
or intend to relinquish, any right or interest she
hath with the other united or confederated States to
the back country . . . . And it is further declared,
That no article in the said Confederation can or
ought to bind this or any other State, to guaranty
any exclusive claim of any particular State to the
soil of the said back lands, or any such claim of
jurisdiction over the said lands, or the inhabitants
thereof." On Washington's birth-day, 1781, the
delegates of Maryland, John Hanson and Daniel
Carroll, took their seats in Congress, with power to
sign the Articles and thus remove the last remain-
ing obstacle to the long-expected Confederation.
The final ratification by the Maryland delegates,
and the announcement of the Articles to the public
was delayed until March 1, 1781, on which day the
delegates from New York formally surrendered to
Congress their claims to the western lands.

There are two facts in connection with this first
legal union of the United States, that deserve men-

tion: The author of the Confederation, John Dickinson, was a Maryland boy, born at Crosia, Talbot County, November 13, 1732; and the first President of the United States of America under the Confederation was John Hanson, also a native of Maryland, and at the time of his election, one of her delegates in Congress.

www.ingramcontent.com/pod-product-compliance
Lightning Source LLC
Chambersburg PA
CBHW022035080426
42733CB00007B/832